EMILY HENSON

Photography by Debi Treloar

Life
UNSTYLED

How to embrace imperfection
and create a home you love.

rps

RYLAND PETERS & SMALL
LONDON • NEW YORK

Festival d'automne à Paris

Dubuffet

Grand
Palais

28 sept. – 20 déc,

29 Novembre

Senior designer Megan Smith
Senior commissioning editor
Annabel Morgan
Location research Jess Walton
and Emily Henson.
Production controller
David Hearn
Art director Leslie Harrington
Editorial director Julia Charles
Publisher Cindy Richards

First published in 2016 by
Ryland Peters & Small
20–21 Jockey's Fields
London WC1R 4BW
and
341 E 116th Street
New York, NY 10029
www.rylandpeters.com

10 9 8 7 6 5 4 3 2 1

ISBN 978-1-84975-754-6

A CIP record for this
book is available from
the British Library.

Library of Congress
CIP data has been
applied for.

Printed and bound
in China

Contents

The idea for *Life Unstyled* was born many years ago, when I started an interiors blog of the same name. As an interior stylist, I create perfectly styled images for my clients in order to sell their products, but the truth is that these pictures don't represent real life. It's all a bit of fiction and fantasy – interiors in a flawless and, frankly, unattainable state, intended to inspire but also setting impossibly high standards of perfection.

My aim for *Life Unstyled* the blog and now this book was to rebel against those spotless, clutter-free interiors and talk instead about real homes, the kind so many of us live in. My mission is to show homes that are not only inspiring and stylish, but also lived in and constantly evolving. As people we are always developing, our likes and dislikes often changing, so it makes sense that our homes should reflect this natural flux.

We live in the age of social media, where we only show the world our best selves – our pretend selves, really. *Life Unstyled* is about feeling good about the way we really live. It is designed to be both an inspiration and a respite – I want to offer you ideas to use at home, and I also want you to sigh with relief when you see that everyone has a tangle of wires and a messy pile of books by their bed, and that it's OK.

In *Life Unstyled*, I celebrate the beauty of imperfect interiors with stories of inspiring homeowners who favour creativity over perfection. My hope is that this book leaves you loving your own home, with all its lumps, bumps and unfinished jobs, just a tiny bit more.

Hidden treasure. When these homeowners removed wallpaper in their apartment, they fell in love with the raw finish left behind (above and opposite). With a coating of sealant, it has as much personality as any wallpaper and is a unique choice. It may not be for everyone, but *Life Unstyled* is about creating a home you love, regardless of what others think.

A home is never done.

Embracing imperfection.

Work with what you've got.

Most people I know have a long list of reasons why their home isn't perfect. Perhaps they're renting, so they can't make their own mark; there isn't a lot of cash to spare for decorating; the space is too small or there isn't enough storage. Perhaps, like me, they work from home and struggle to carve out a work area. Few of us feel that our home fulfills our every need and – let's be honest – that's a pretty tall order to begin with. But there are creative ways to tackle many of these issues, and in this chapter I highlight some of my favourite solutions from homeowners who have overcome various challenges.

Often it just comes down to attitude – we need to train ourselves to see the opportunities rather than the problems. So instead of lamenting the fact that you can't warm yourself by your defunct fireplace, why not fill it with flowers and candles and congratulate yourself on your creativity and resourcefulness? There's nothing wrong with striving for more, but it's also important to make the most of what you've got.

Why don't you...
Create an impromptu display case from a non-working fireplace by filling it with things you love? Here, buckets of dried flowers and a tray of pillar candles do the trick (above).

On display. No space for a home office? It may be possible to tuck a workspace into the corner of your living area, as this jewellery designer has done (left). An inexpensive plastic trestle table is hidden beneath Dutch wax fabric, above which hangs a photo of the Great Wall of China by artist Sarah Charlesworth. A white tabletop rests on vintage wooden cabinets, creating a wide desk as well as a display area for photos and collections (opposite).

Small spaces. In this sixth-floor flat (above), space is at a premium. The corner beneath a window was put to good use by building a custom bench from birch ply. It's a small area that could have gone to waste, but now it doubles as seating and much-needed storage. This small bay window (above right) is too narrow to accommodate a sofa, so a pair of petite upholstered armchairs and stools do the job instead. Kitchen cupboards were in short supply here (right), so this homeowner sought out vintage trolleys on wheels to hold overflow pots and pans.

Kids at work. The tenants of this Parisian apartment move frequently, so rather than filling up their kids' rooms with bulky items of furniture, they grouped together an odd collection of small tables (some bought for two euros apiece) to make a multi-level, movable LEGO-building station.

Tucked away. Under the stairs, in a space that could have been filled with bikes and boxes, hides an artist/carpenter's office furnished with mismatched tables and offering plenty of room to experiment (this page). A teen's platform bed is built into a small loft space, chunky shelves doubling as stairs (opposite).

Signs of life.

The homes that interest me are stylish, creative and inspiring, but also brimming with evidence that people actually live there. I don't know about you, but I'm tired of seeing photos of bedside tables holding only an artfully placed pair of reading glasses and a carafe of water instead of the stacks of books, notepads and odds and ends we all know should be there. Or the bathroom shelf decorated with one spotless bottle of designer hand soap and little else.

What I like to see is a tangle of wires under a desk, a fridge plastered with bills and letters from school and a pile of shoes by the front door. This is real life for most of us, and doesn't it feel good to be reminded that we aren't alone in our imperfect homes? We might not choose to share this less-than-perfect reality on social media, opting instead for a more 'edited' (ahem, fake) version of reality, but in truth life can be untidy and that's OK. Don't be taken in by the perceived perfection that's thrust upon us everywhere we turn.

In this section, I hope to inspire you to stop worrying about the piles of papers on the kitchen table and the overflowing junk drawer and to offer a few solutions for wrangling life's inevitable messes. Most importantly, I hope you'll be a bit more gentle on yourself and remember that nobody's home is perfect.

Nothing to hide. These homeowners share the philosophy that, if they own it, why hide it? The London warehouse of an art collector and writer is filled with pieces loved by the owner, mostly in a natural, earthy palette. Shelves above the kitchen counter are crammed with pots, vases, teapots and ceramics of every kind (above and left). In a tiny South London kitchen (above left), open shelving showcases this pretty collection of plates and glassware. A lack of wardrobe/closet space forced this homeowner to store her clothes on a rolling clothes rack in the bedroom (opposite far left)

Why don't you...

Keep a collection of small pots and tins to
catch the coins, batteries, rubber bands and
stray paper clips that are always, always around
(below)? Once in a while, empty, sort and put
away. In the meantime, let it go.

Contained. In this Belgian bathroom, toiletries are kept on display but corralled in Perspex boxes and a tall red plastic tower of trays (opposite above left). Wooden crates are tucked into a discreet corner of this London kitchen. Cookbooks are stored within, while on top a family charging station keeps phones, tablets and their annoying cables all in one place (opposite above right). This bookcase holds more than just books – toys, snow globes and other knick-knacks clutter it up beautifully (left).

19

Colourful corners.
In this rented Parisian apartment, the owners have made their mark with bold wallpaper and paint in the bijou kitchen, turning a door into a pinboard to showcase kids' art and family photos (left). In the bedroom, books are stacked up beside the bed and a home office space is tucked into a corner (opposite).

Keep it natural. In the Brooklyn home of a prop stylist and a fashion editor, collections are all around (below and opposite). The walls above the work area are pinned with odds and ends that catch their eye, but what ties it all together are the natural tones – sepia photographs, shell spoons, samples of different shades of linen, brass sculptures and beads. When disparate items are grouped with purpose, they can create a cabinet of curiosities and an intriguing window to the collector's mind.

This isn't a section (or a book, for that matter) for minimalists. On these pages is everything you need to feel good about all life's bits and pieces – the random trinkets that your kids insist on hoarding, the china you can't stop collecting, the tools of your trade that you need to keep close to hand and the books you've read but can't part with.

Whether we live alone or as part of a family, we all know how easy it is to accumulate stuff. Only the most disciplined of us can claim otherwise. I tend to amass a lot because of my job as a stylist, but I don't have everything out on display at once. Instead, I rotate collections as my mood changes and as I acquire new bits, stashing the rest in plastic bins in my basement.

To create a more pleasing and cohesive visual story with favourite items of clutter, it helps to group them by theme, colour or material. Make use of any spare wall space or open shelves, or, if you're lucky enough to have them, take advantage of glass-fronted cabinets to corral your collections. And remember, there are no rules about what you can collect, so costume jewellery, vintage postcards and piles of pretty rocks all have a place.

Good clutter.

Why don't you...

Découpage your bookshelves with pages from books or magazines instead of painting them (below)? Wrap the shelves in pages that you find appealing, secure them with PVA glue and then varnish them for a clean, smooth finish.

Anything goes. White ceramics are stored in a glass-fronted cabinet, standing out beautifully against the dark background – a collection like this deserves its own cupboard (below). In a London kitchen, birch plywood shelves are stained black and dressed with teapots, plates and bowls, proving that open shelving doesn't have to be perfectly styled to look interesting (below left). An artist's tools of the trade (including toothbrushes!) are easily within reach in beakers on his desk (left). Young children often amass lots of bits and pieces – drawings, little toys, things made at nursery – and it makes them feel good if they can proudly display them in their rooms (opposite above and below). I've never been precious about what my kids choose to display and how they do it, allowing them creative freedom in their own spaces.

Embracing colour. In the Brussels home studio of a set decorator and graphic designer, one wall has been given over to a colourful collection of art, some of it made by the owner. The pieces are linked by bold colour and texture, with black and white frames grounding the tactile collection.

Paint is your friend.

I think the phrase 'a lotta bang for your buck' was created for paint. Little else can transform a room as quickly, easily and inexpensively. You don't need special skills, as with hanging wallpaper, yet you can make a huge impact in very little time. A room with an interesting paint treatment can get away with a multitude of sins – the eye is distracted from day-to-day clutter and drawn instead to whatever inspired paint job you think up, whether it's two-toned walls or rainbow-coloured stairs.

Gone are the days of adhering to rules when it comes to using paint at home – if you can imagine it, you can paint it. And the worst-case scenario is, of course, that you don't like the results – in which event you repaint. It can be as simple and quick as spray-painting the legs of a stool or as complicated and time-consuming as creating an intricate geometric design on a blank wall. In this section, I've compiled some of my favourite creative ideas to suit those wanting to gently test the waters, as well as others for those who are feeling a bit more adventurous.

Why don't you...

Imitate this thrifty homeowner and use an upturned wooden crate as a bedside table, first giving it a lick of bright paint to suit your taste (above)? A can of spray paint makes quick work of reinventing small items at little cost.

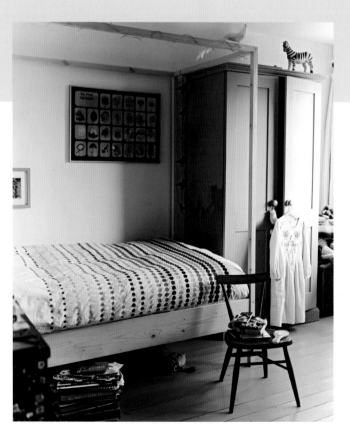

Bright beneath your feet. I love a painted floor, whether it's in the shape of wooden floorboards like this girl's bedroom (left) or the old linoleum flooring in the Belgian studio (opposite). Choosing a bright colour is a surefire way to create instant interest in a room, but if it seems too extreme you could opt for something softer, such as a pale blue or sage green. Painting a floor is a good way to conceal scuffed wood or outdated tiles. Of course, it will itself scuff over time, but it's nice, 'artistic' scuffing, so we don't mind as much. Adds character, right?

Be bold. Despite being renters, these Parisians went to town with paint. They were given some coloured velvet by a friend and made it into sofa cushions (opposite). This left the white wall behind looking bare, hence the bold painted geometric design. In the kitchen, the ceiling and wood beams were also given a lick of vibrant turquoise paint (right).

Why don't you...

Paint your stairs in a rainbow of colours, like this French family did (above)? Stairs tend to be overlooked but are often the first thing you see when you enter a home. It's an easy way to update worn wooden treads in older homes.

Something for everyone. Venetian plaster tinted a soft peachy pink makes a world of difference in this London flat (left), and features frequently in the florist owner's stunning photos of her blooms. In Brooklyn, the bohemian homeowners went for chalky pastels for their living room wall and the inside of their front door (opposite below right). Flat black paint looks especially striking when French doors are painted the same. The wooden chopping boards look like sculptures against the dark backdrop (opposite below left). Both the bathtub and walls are painted shades of orange in this jewel box of a bathroom (opposite above left).

33

Break the rules.

This book is all about breaking the rules and finding your own way in the world of interiors. In this section in particular, I want to encourage you to challenge the way that things are done and to ask yourself if you can come up with something better.

I've always liked doing things my own way when it comes to my home, not concerning myself too much with predictions for next year's trends or the right way to hang curtains. Many of the homeowners I met during the making of this book felt the same way. Their only concern was to create a home that was right for them, regardless of what tradition dictates. For one couple, this meant painting only half a wall to expose the patina of the raw plaster above. For another homeowner, it meant using museum archive units for storage. These decisions defy convention and that's what makes them stand out. It takes guts to dismiss the traditional ways of doing things, but if you can't please yourself in your own home, where can you?

Why don't you...

Refresh a piece of furniture at your local car body shop? This resourceful homeowner bought a damaged fibreglass chair and had the broken section patched and then sprayed a glossy, pristine white (left).

Against the grain. Before the advent of plasterboard/ drywall, lath and plaster walls were the norm, the lath (thin strips of wood) being covered in plaster. This homeowner took this idea and flipped it on its head, using rough lath as a wall finish (above). The stairs in the entrance of a converted warehouse were intentionally left unpainted to reference the history of the building (opposite). A Veronese mural from Surface View contrasts with a 20th-century fibreglass chair in this home office (left).

Think different. In this home, the 'dead' space at the top of the stairs has been put to good use with the addition of a pair of bookcases (above). Hallways, landings and awkward spaces are all good places for slotting in more storage. Try looking at your home with fresh eyes and see the opportunities. In this teen's room (right), a vintage glass and metal cabinet is used to hold clothes rather than kitchenware or decorative accessories. And a scuffed, painted newel post is an unlikely partner for this contemporary staircase (above right), a welcome reminder that contrasting elements keep things interesting.

Halfway there. Rather than painting over their raw plastered walls, these owners stopped halfway, leaving the patina of the plaster on the upper walls exposed. Taking full advantage of the vast ceiling height, a drop of wallpaper has been hung on one wall for a dramatic effect. This is such a clever trick for renters or anyone who is unable to commit to wallpaper.

Eccentric warehouse.
Rows of archive cabinets, typically used in museums, glide along tracks and house everything from dinner plates and ceramic collections to clothes (opposite). To divide up this huge open-plan space, lengths of fabric, hand-printed by the owner, hang from bars, adding privacy and interest (right).

Clever reinventions. These chunky kitchen shelves were made from heavy wooden planks saved during this home's renovation (left). Long nails have been hammered into the edges and used as hooks. This eclectic London home (opposite) is full of ideas for creative reuse. The sofa is brightened up with a quilt, adding colour and pattern as well as covering wear and tear. The coffee table was made from the centre section of a dining table found in a skip/dumpster and made mobile with the addition of wheels.

Why don't you...

Make your own pendant light? Here (below), a hole was drilled in the bottom of a plastic bucket for a flex cord, then a light fitting plus a low-wattage bulb was added.

In this disposable age, where the lifespan of furniture is getting shorter and shorter, anything we can save from landfill is a bonus. Whether it's for the sake of our planet or for the pleasure of making something new from something old, being creative before you consume is a worthy pursuit. I look at it as a win-win-win situation: I save money, I don't produce as much waste and I create a unique item for myself.

Creativity before consumption is about reinvention and customization. I get a huge amount of satisfaction from having something that no one else does, so personalizing my home is important. With some imagination, you can find ways to revive tired, unloved pieces and put your own stamp on your home.

It's easy to just buy stuff. It takes a little more time and thought to create a one-off, but the reward is so much greater. Whether you spruce up a worn sofa with a patterned throw or you make your own pendants from painted papier mâché, creativity before consumption results in a uniquely personal home.

Creativity before consumption.

Ideas to steal. This old school science lab cupboard was previously used as a toy cupboard and then as a living-room bookcase (above). Now, with the doors removed and a blank internal door fitted as a desktop, it has become a bookcase and crafting area in a girl's bedroom. This quirky cabinet has been in the family for years (right). Cut-outs were made in the once-solid timber doors, and legs from an old coffee table were added and made over with yellow electrical tape. The fascia of a child's bed (above right) was constructed from old garden fencing.

The many faces of plywood. A large piece of wallpapered plywood leans on the wall behind the sofa in this Brooklyn loft (left). This is a clever idea if you don't have a sufficient quantity of vintage wallpaper to cover a room or if you want to have the effect of wallpaper without the expense or commitment. A stylish budget kitchen makeover wows with black-stained birch plywood cabinets and utilitarian taps/faucets made from a length of copper piping (above).

An instant headboard.
Make your own 'headboard' by painting a piece of neutral fabric. Here (right), silver paint was roughly applied to a large piece of inexpensive muslin/cheesecloth and then pinned to the wall. The end effect should look spontaneous and rough around the edges, which makes it a less intimidating project to tackle. Aim for charming imperfection, and you can't go wrong!

Handmade everything. Bright ideas from a family who likes to put their stamp on absolutely everything – a philosophy I share. A linen sack has been dyed green and tied shut with string and handmade pompoms (above left) – an easy-to-copy cushion idea you could recreate with a store-bought pillowcase. In the family bathroom, the washing machine is tucked in a corner and hidden behind a piece of vintage fabric, which is simply folded over and clipped onto a length of wire strung between two walls (left). These paper pendant lights were made by layering decorative papier mâché over metal pendants and allowing it to dry before removing (above).

People live here.

Handmade
HAVEN

IN THE CENTRE OF THE SOUTHERN FRENCH CITY OF NIMES, this breathtaking apartment occupies the second storey of a building that dates back to 1885. With its double-height ceilings and stone floors the home strikes an intimidating pose, but thanks to the eclectic taste and creativity of its owners Myriam and Dominique Balaÿ, it feels inviting and warm.

Myriam, Dominique and their daughters Alix and Zoe, aged 16 and 14, have lived here for seven years now, having traded in their hectic Parisian lives for a slower-paced existence close to the mountains and sea. Even with two teenagers, there is an enviable amount of space for the family to spread out and enjoy their creative pursuits.

A textile designer by trade, Myriam's creativity knows no bounds. At various points in their careers, she and Dominique designed props and sets for TV, film and theatre, textiles for fashion brands including Issey Miyake and

Faded grandeur. The raw plaster finish on the walls throughout this French home gives it an air of faded grandeur; a perfect foil to the homeowners' brightly coloured textiles and art (opposite and above). Remnants of a handmade paper garland are strung onto a vintage metal wall sconce (above right). The unusual low sofa is made up of a pile of thin, fabric-covered mattresses piled high with cushions sewn by the owner and is flanked by white curtains made from printed Tyvek (above left).

Personalize it. Every effort has been made to customize in this home. The sofa and chairs have been covered with boldly patterned fabric and arranged beneath the art-hung walls of the living room. Myriam's penchant for the handmade is evident in a makeshift coat hook (above right) and papier mâché pendant lights (above). She used metal lampshades (an inflated balloon also works) as a mould, layering on papier mâché and cutting a hole for the cord. Once dry, she gave them a paint finish – splatters, brushstrokes, drips – fitted them with a low wattage bulb and hung from a hook.

Nicole Farhi and stunning handmade paper lamps for private clients and their own interiors shop. While they no longer have a store, evidence of the couple's prolific creative output is everywhere in their home.

It's always a treat to see the different ways in which people choose to decorate and it's especially inspiring when homeowners ignore the rules and do the unexpected. This home is grand in its proportions, with high ceilings, big rooms and large windows letting in that gorgeous southern light. It could have gone glossy and slick. Instead, Myriam and Dominique have allowed the space to remain raw and rough, a look that works perfectly when combined with pops of bright colour, patterned textiles and a mix of vintage and found furniture and accessories.

When they moved in, the couple set to work removing 80 years' worth of bad taste – false ceilings, linoleum and outdated wallpaper. Some rooms were repainted, including the kitchen, bathroom and bedrooms, but on most of the

walls the rough finish of the patched plaster was left bare – a bold choice. At first glance, this resembles wallpaper, tricking the eye into seeing a pattern where none exists. It's not a look that will appeal to everyone, but the plaster adds visual interest to the vast rooms and serves as a distinctive backdrop for the artwork and furniture.

Myriam is a maker, and one of the most striking features about this home is that so much is handmade. Everything has a story, whether it's a chair that was found on the street and updated, a paper lampshade that's one of Myriam's own creations or a mesh vegetable sack, stuffed and turned into a decorative cushion. It's all had a sprinkle of the Myriam gold dust and that's what makes it feel unique. One large room is devoted to the couple's creativity and business. Myriam's newest endeavour is loom bracelets, launched in 2015 and sold internationally. In the home studio, her loom is set up, ready to weave her indigo-dyed and metallic threads into one-of-a-kind creations.

Storage galore. In the home office, a large dresser/hutch was painted black and topped with a chalkboard for to-do lists and reminders. A towering stack of vintage suitcases provides extra storage space for textiles and other materials needed for Myriam and Dominique's creations (left).

CREATIVITY BEFORE CONSUMPTION.
In the kitchen, a simple hook has been fashioned from scrap wood and hung high on the wall, where its bright orange hue pops against the soft green walls (below). It's an idea that's easily recreated: any scrap of wood can be painted and mounted with a metal hook.

While there isn't a strict colour theme running throughout the home, colour plays an important role. There's pink, green, orange, purple and yellow – you name it, it's here. Textiles also feature heavily, which is not surprising given Myriam's history with textile design. There are vintage floral prints, hand-dyed linen, painted muslin/cheesecloth and even Tyvek all vying for attention. It shouldn't work, but it does.

I'm not sure what I would do with so much space. On the one hand, it's a dream scenario – spare rooms! A place to permanently set up the sewing machine! Entire cupboards just for fabric collections! But on the other hand, managing a huge space is not an easy feat to get right, and rooms of this scale can feel empty and cold. But with creativity and bravery, the Balaÿ clan have infused their home with an abundance of personality, and it feels alive, loved and lived in.

Mismatched. In the high-ceilinged kitchen, one wall has been given a coat of pale green paint that contrasts vividly with the terracotta tiled floors. A colourful mismatched collection of chairs surrounds the table and the walls are dotted with coat hooks that hold frequently used items such as mesh shopping bags.

Work life. Myriam and Dominique run their business from home, so have dedicated one room to their office and craft atelier. Here, floor-to-ceiling industrial shelving is stuffed with everything they need and covered with a curtain to conceal the chaos. In the centre of the room is a handsome black table where, at any given time, some form of creative industry is taking place. A loom for making Myriam's woven cotton bracelets sits alongside a multi-level intray – something we should all invest in to control the endless piles of papers (opposite). Dotted around the office, and elsewhere in the home, are baskets of textiles, coloured cottons and yarn, the tools of Myriam and Dominique's trade (this page).

Every home should have...

Bookshelves like these. These stacked shelves tell me that this is a family who actually reads. There are no perfectly colour-coordinated spines or little trinkets or vases expertly styled in with the piles of books. These are shelves that are used and books that are read, and that's just the way I like it (right).

Well read. There's nothing more comforting than an hardworking bookshelf. Here, books are haphazardly piled high on shelves that have been découpaged with pages from books and magazines (above). In this bedroom, there is a cheerful mix of rumpled linen bedding in clashing colours and papier mâché lights handmade by Myriam. A basket perched on a canvas stool makes a useful bedside catch-all (left). In the master bedroom, the wall was only painted partway up and a bamboo window blind was transformed into a headboard with yellow paint and hung horizontally (right).

Perfectly imperfect. In the kitchen, the beautiful wooden cabinets and handles were made by Daniel and some friends. The yellow and white floor tiles were laid in a slightly uneven manner, which adds to the character of the space (opposite). Planks left over from the renovation were reused as shelves, with nails hammered into the edges to create cup hooks (above). A collection of patterned bowls store garlic and ginger (right).

Bohemian
BROWNSTONE

IN GREENPOINT, BROOKLYN'S NORTHERN-MOST NEIGHBOURHOOD, Sybil Domond and Daniel Lessin have set up their business and their home mere blocks from one another, and in the process have created a little bohemian community where their young family can thrive.

Sybil and Daniel own People of 2morrow, a boutique specializing in clothing and home accessories with a bohemian spin. Daniel also co-owns Bembe, a thriving bar in Williamsburg that draws crowds for its mojitos and tiny but packed dance floor. As well as running the store, Sybil also dabbles in interior design, which comes as no surprise when you see her talent for creating a relaxed, bohemian environment infused with personality.

The couple bought this three-storey 1890 brick townhouse in 2008 and have been renovating it ever since. They currently live on the top floor with their five-year-old daughter, but plan to

move down to the ground floor, which offers access to the garden and the potential to dig out the basement. Rather than occupying the whole building, the entrepreneurial couple have cleverly designed each floor as a self-contained apartment, renting the other two out via Airbnb.

Despite this being a complete gut job, the apartment doesn't feel polished and perfect like many renovations, a fact I appreciate. Because of the materials chosen it is characterful and comfortable, as if Sybil and Daniel have lived there for years – and that takes skill. Just like their club Bembe, where most of the materials used for the interior were salvaged, the couple reused whatever they could when they renovated. Wooden planks were recycled as open shelving in the kitchen, and brickwork and wooden beams were left raw and exposed.

Thanks to the lofty ceiling height in the top-floor flat, Sybil and Daniel were able to build a mezzanine level where they sleep, beneath which their daughter has her own bedroom and play area. This isn't a large home, but smart decisions about furniture and storage mean that it feels surprisingly spacious. Rather than trying to fit in a large sofa, which would have eaten up precious floor space, a cosy nook was designed at the back of the apartment; an L-shaped bench piled with cushions and with storage space beneath. We visited in winter, when the trees were bare. But sitting there in the summer months, with trees in full leaf, it must feel like being in a tree house. Just across from the sofa nook, in the kitchen, wooden cabinets were designed and built by Daniel and some talented friends, adding further authenticity to an already unique home.

Touch of the hand. The apartment is blessed with high ceilings that are put to good use by hanging pots and pans and a variety of pendant lights from the rafters. The windows at the back were custom-made by Daniel and friends, and bring in an exceptional amount of light (opposite). A small collection of plants and crystals rests atop a dresser/hutch (above), and on the wall behind the oven rests a painted shutter, purchased from an artist selling on the street (right).

Aside from a few IKEA purchases, the furniture and accessories were mostly handmade by local artists, bought at estate sales or collected on the couple's travels. Sybil's talent for curating a unique collection for her boutique came in handy when decorating their home, and her access to emerging designers and artists was invaluable. The walls are hung with handmade weavings and dotted around are collections of crystals and trinkets – many of them also found in their boutique. When the couple travel, it has become a tradition for them to bring back a special textile as a souvenir. Their shared love of textiles can be seen in the diverse collection of cushions and the lengths of fabric hung in place of wardrobe/closet doors.

On the walls, bold colours have been used to great effect. In the main living area, one wall is painted two shades of minty green, while the back of the front door directly next to it is a pastel pink, all hand-mixed by the couple. The same method was employed in the cosy nook area, with one wall painted in blocks of blue. These colour choices work well against the rougher elements in the apartment, like the brick and wood, and the matt finish prevents the paint from looking too glossy and slick.

Perhaps because Daniel and Sybil have worked on their home over many years, it has a beautifully relaxed and authentic feeling about it. It doesn't feel overly designed. If anything, it feels spontaneously put together rather than rigidly planned. For me this is what building a great home is all about – evolving and developing slowly over time, because often the best ideas only reveal themselves once you've lived in a space.

Secret storage. Salvaged wood shelves were added to the brick wall in Sybil and Daniel's daughter's room and are now home to her art supplies, toys and books. A pendant light made from a dried gourd casts a warm glow at night (right). Next to the kitchen is a seating area with views to the trees outside. The seats of the L-shaped bench lift to reveal storage space. The wooden wall to the right is in fact a large sliding door behind which hides a wardrobe/closet. A bohemian blend of cushions and textiles contrasts with the exposed brick wall and the strip of two-tone plaster (opposite).

CREATIVITY BEFORE CONSUMPTION

So much is custom-built or repurposed in this home that it's hard to choose what to talk about! In this room alone, the couple built a mezzanine level for their bedroom, converted upturned metal baskets into novel light fixtures and opted for a striped hammock rather than a bulky sofa – a clever idea for small-space living (below).

Bare brick. The exposed brickwork that runs throughout the apartment provides a textured and soulful backdrop for the family's eclectic collections of art and accessories. Up on the mezzanine level, the master bedroom is a simple affair, with a cosy low-slung bed and a pair of yellow IKEA stools used as bedside tables (above). In the bathroom the brickwork continues, broken only by a row of vivid green tiles (right). Beneath the couple's mezzanine bedroom is their daughter's bedroom and play area (opposite), a playful feast for the eyes, decorated in a fun and haphazard way with strings of lights, colourful art, a painted zebra head and a cluster of beads and pompoms collected on their travels (above right).

Wanderlust IN PARIS

RAMDANE TOUHAMI AND VICTOIRE DE TAILLAC-TOUHAMI
ARE SERIAL ENTREPRENEURS and self-proclaimed gypsies
who hop continents every few years in the endless pursuit of
a full life. Home for now is a rented apartment in Paris's 7th
arrondissement, with a view of the Eiffel Tower and plenty
of room for their three children, Scherazade, aged 13, Adam, 11,
and Noor, 8, to grow.

Occupying the top two floors of an 18th-century building
in the heart of one of Paris's most elegant and exclusive
neighbourhoods, one might expect this family home to boast
a slick, buttoned-up interior. Instead, the Touhami clan's
creativity runs riot, from the boldly wallpapered rooms and
multicoloured stair treads to the tongue-in-cheek artwork
and nonchalantly displayed collections.

Ramdane has been designing since he was a teenager,
launching a T-shirt line aged 17 and working ceaselessly ever
since in the worlds of fashion, art, design, home fragrance
and beauty. His attention to detail, commitment to quality
and flair for branding are the reasons some of us are willing
to part with a small fortune for a scented candle. Ramdane was
previously CEO and co-owner of Cire Trudon, a 17th-century
luxury candle brand that he helped to revive and which is now
sold in 58 countries. Today with Victoire, formerly PR for Paris
boutique Colette and now a specialist in skincare and the
science of traditional and natural beauty, he is doing the same

Beautiful chaos. The living room may boast views
of the Eiffel Tower, but it is far from pretentious.
Classic chairs, most found at antiques fairs or
given by family, are grouped in a sociable cluster.
The bookshelves are comfortingly chaotic,
evidence that the books are actually read.

Brights and lights. Rather than arranging your typical sofa and armchairs around the fireplace, Ramdane and Victoire have opted for a decorative metal daybed and a collection of vintage chairs. An upturned barrel, painted red, makes a sturdy side table (opposite). Who says you have to choose between colour and whitewash? Both looks literally sit side by side here, the whites making the brights stand out even more (this page).

Rich hues. Deep shades of paint, wallpaper and upholstery bring a rich moodiness to some rooms. On one dining-room wall is a geometric wallpaper by Cole & Son (above left), on another a sultry aubergine paint, all the better for displaying wax busts, vintage chemists' bottles and books on natural remedies (opposite). A family portrait by friend Artus de Lavilléon hangs in the master bedroom (above).

thing for Buly 1803, an 18th-century perfumer. With a breathtaking shop on rue Bonaparte in Paris plus a space in London's fashion-forward Dover Street Market and more stores planned in the near future, as well as a book about natural beauty secrets from around the globe and *Corpus*, a magazine they publish about beauty, body and mind, this is one very busy couple. Somehow they have also found the time to create a captivating home.

With their children in tow, the couple spent two years living in Tangier and two in Brooklyn before returning to Paris in 2012, where they found this stunning apartment. In all three cities, the family decorated their home with

roughly the same assortment of furniture, picking up a few new pieces to add to the mix each time. I've seen photos of each home and it's fascinating to see the same things in completely different settings. Their home is furnished with a mix of antique, designer and family pieces combined with artwork and creative flourishes, giving it a wonderfully eclectic vibe.

The Touhamis seem to have a knack for finding rented homes with personality, but they also make the effort to add their own personal touches. I find this attitude inspiring. I used to believe it was a waste of money to paint or wallpaper a rented home that you might only occupy for

a limited amount of time. But the Touhamis always customize each rental, because they want to enjoy it while it's their home. No matter where they go, they strive to recreate, as Victoire describes it, 'their world'.

If you're renting, wallpaper and paint are investments on which you won't see a return, but they will increase your 'daily happiness factor' (shall we call it DHF?), which is surely just as important. Our homes influence our moods, for better or worse, so surrounding ourselves with our own version of beauty should be a priority wherever we live.

Personal touches abound in the Touhami household, as well as a reassuring amount of real-life stuff – piles of books, LEGO spread out over a cluster of tiny tables, shelves bulging with photos, toys and knick-knacks, none of it styled or arranged in any particular fashion. Just the way I like it. Each room tells its own story, with different colours and prints and no apparent thread linking them, aside from that of a happy-go-lucky, creative family.

What I took away from this home and its occupants is that we should strive to make a home wherever we are and for however long we plan to stay, rather than waiting for some unspecified time in the future when we have our 'dream' house. Our surroundings should inspire and invigorate us, whether we live in a Parisian penthouse or a basement flat in the dodgy part of town, so whatever your situation, be sure to make the place your own.

Kids' space. On one side of this shared boy/girl bedroom is a collection of tables covered with LEGO. On the other is a doll's house (opposite). Call it stereotypical, but the lines have been drawn. Boys and girls can easily share a room when they're young, each getting their own corner. Ramdane commissioned the paintings of Hello Kitty's imagined ancestors for the brand's 25-year anniversary. Their older daughter claims her space with hand-drawn messages tacked to the wall (above).

An area to tack up anything and everything that inspires. The wall above Victoire's desk is covered with an assortment of photos, postcards and art (opposite). It's important to have a place to display the things you love.

Collected treasures. In the master bedroom, an elegant metal canopy bed holds court, topped with a crown and decked out in a soft floral quilt. On either side are two tall metal and mirrored Indian screens, part of a trio bought at a store in Paris. The vintage fabric of the bedspread and the floral mattresses piled beneath the bed make the room less grand and more of a cosy retreat for the whole family (right). In the master bathroom, the couple keep their toiletries out on display, as well as framed photos and art. The large painted wooden tub under the sink is for used towels (above).

More is more. In this open-plan loft, wooden tables are grouped together to divide the kitchen from the dining area and to provide a surface for displaying favourite things (opposite). Next to the fridge the cubbies of a low bookcase are filled with crockery (above), while the top acts as a bar. The kitchen is small and basic but given personality with a large painting and fabric curtains (right).

Eclectic
RIVERSIDE FACTORY

JUST A FEW BLOCKS FROM BOTH THE MANHATTAN BRIDGE AND THE BROOKLYN BRIDGE, prop stylist Martin Bourne and fashion editor Leilin Lopez share this eclectic loft in a 19th-century factory building that was formerly the New York Coffee Exchange. Situated in DUMBO, one of the most sought-after neighbourhoods in Brooklyn, the couple's home is filled with stylish ideas and inspiration for living with the things you love.

    For those not in the know, DUMBO – an acronym for Down Under the Manhattan Bridge Overpass – has been one of New York's premier arts districts for some time. The double-edged sword that is gentrification has driven out many of the artists who originally made the area desirable, and DUMBO is now one of the most expensive locations in New York, with an influx of developers building luxury apartments. This second-floor 185-square-metre/2000-square-foot

Make an entrance. Martin inherited the large wooden unit with the loft and gave it a coat of milky green paint to freshen it up. Now, placed directly near the entrance, it is a handy catch-all unit for books, CDs and a collection of glass vases (left). The unit is also home to a pair of old wooden washboards from Africa that are perfect for displaying small collections, as the ridges prevent small items from rolling away (above).

loft has been Martin's home since he moved from London to New York 20 years ago. The building was given 'artist loft' status in 2000, which means it has both residential and commercial status and the rent is controlled. In a nutshell, Martin and Leilin won the New York renter's lottery.

Warehouse living is my dream. I used to want a big rambling house, slightly ramshackle, with lots of rooms and peeling wallpaper, but in recent years my vision has changed. A huge open space like Martin and Leilin's would be incredible, and seeing the way they have divided the space up into designated areas – kitchen, dining, living, working and sleeping – is inspiring. It may seem contradictory to include the home of a well-known stylist in a book entitled *Life Unstyled*, but stylists have so much to share in terms of how to make your home personal in a way that feels natural.

One of Martin's mantras is that if you love something you can find a way to make it work in your space. When he moved to New York, he brought very little with him from England: an African stool, a wind-up gramophone player and a beautiful lichen-covered terracotta vase that he still uses today. Over the years Martin and Leilin have built up an impressive collection of art, furniture and mementoes, shopping regularly at Brooklyn's flea markets as well as picking up objects on their travels. The upside to living in such a large space, with a calming palette of whites, soft blues and grey on the walls and floors, is that you can collect to your heart's content. All manner of bits and bobs line the walls and most surfaces, as one would expect in the home of a stylist (we see everything as a potential prop, so it's hard to say no), but because of the high ceilings and open layout, the space doesn't feel cluttered.

Flexible seating that can be easily moved
around to accommodate changing needs.
A combination of different chairs, pouffes
and stools is often more practical than a
large sofa and armchairs (below).

One of the first things Martin did upon moving in was to remove the 40 fluorescent tubes that lit the space and which were controlled by just a single switch – either all off or all on! He painted the plywood floors a pale grey-blue and, a year after moving in, decided to build two rooms in the open-plan space, using existing columns to mark out the footprint of each room. Choosing inexpensive wooden subflooring material for the walls, Martin constructed a pair of bedrooms, cleverly designing them with wardrobes/closets built on the exterior rather than the interior, allowing each room to feel uncluttered and calm, a place just for rest.

The basic layout of the furniture in the loft doesn't change that frequently, but smaller pieces are often moved around. The extra-long dining table was built in situ by a friend, Martin's idea being that he wanted three long planks on legs. The wooden planks were hoisted up one by one through the elevator shaft, and if Martin and Leilin move, the table will have to stay. Sometimes it's piled high with collections of books, vases and various objects, while at other times it is adorned with just one huge vase of flowering branches.

Creating a Life Unstyled doesn't mean styling is not allowed. The trick is to imitate professional stylists and keep on styling, changing things regularly and playing with different combinations of your possessions. Train your eye to appreciate the obscure, not just the obviously beautiful. Hung on the walls among Martin and Leilin's photography and art are objects that some might consider trash – crumpled bundles of rusted wire, once used to bind bales of hay, now hang on nails like tiny metal sculptures. Old wooden washboards from Africa display seemingly disparate objects collected over the years – key chains, unusual pens, badges, a string of wooden beads. Because if it's beautiful to you, then it's beautiful. End of story.

Calming palette. Martin and Leilin have not adhered to a strict colour palette in the loft, with green, pink, lavender, red and blue shades coexisting harmoniously. All these colours are grounded by the pale floors and natural wood furniture. The extra-long dining table was custom-built on site by a friend (opposite). The bedroom is small and dark, a snug space for relaxation. The brick walls were painted and the wall behind the bed hung salon style with an assortment of framed art (above).

CREATIVITY BEFORE CONSUMPTION

Martin and Leilin created desks and work stations
in one corner of the loft. Rather than settling for
dull office furniture, dark wood cabinets and more
contemporary white units were topped with long
countertops. Keep your eye out for old doors or
tabletops, both of which make good desks when
mounted on top of a pair of low cabinets.

Collect, display, repeat. There's enough space in the loft for a number of work stations. One is home to a laptop and printer (above), another is adorned with a rotating collection of objects and art that inspires (opposite, left and above left), and a third has drawers for office supplies. Two of the desktops were made by stapling canvas to sheets of plywood and finishing the edges with upholstery nails (left and above). Martin and Leilin also created additional storage for the less attractive things we all accumulate, like empty suitcases and boxes of memorabilia, and hung a curtain to keep it all out of view (above).

Layered LUXE

IT'S SAFE TO SAY THAT KRISTIAN LAZZARO has one of the most enviable interiors-related jobs around, as Anthropologie's Senior Buyer for furniture, lighting, curtains, rugs and antique furniture. That shibori-dyed sofa and rattan bed you've been coveting? Kristian made that happen, along with so many other swoonworthy pieces. A buyer by profession and a self-confessed shopper by nature, seeing what Kristian has chosen for his own home was fascinating. How does he edit? Does he stick to one style, one colour scheme? How does he stop himself from buying everything he sees on his globetrotting buying trips?

Kristian's three-story row house in Philadelphia's hip up-and-coming Fishtown neighbourhood is testament to his impeccable taste and his innate ability to mix styles and eras in a way that feels layered and interesting rather than cluttered and overwhelming.

Fit for a gentleman. Kristian's living room is a lesson in 'more is more'. Anchored by a leather Chesterfield found on Craigslist and a wooden mantel bought at a flea market, the room is a rich and luxurious collection of very beautiful things, arranged in a way that beckons you to come and sit, relax, maybe sip a Scotch. The antique Chinese wooden screens in the windows were found covered with tattered rice paper, which Kristian removed (above and opposite).

Vintage remix. The kitchen had very little cabinetry, so Kristian supplemented it with a number of freestanding pieces. Two trolleys on wheels, one new and one vintage, hold platters and bowls, and a glass-fronted cabinet stores a variety of ceramics and china, easily available for daily use.

Built in 1915, the home became his when he moved to Philadelphia to begin working at Anthropologie's head office. Kristian lived in New York City for 11 years, a city that's notorious for cramped apartment living, so for him the prospect of owning an entire house was thrilling. The property had already been brought up to date by a developer, but it's the unexpected features added by Kristian that give this home personality and heart. With its highly polished floors and brand new quartz worksurfaces, this house could have gone in the direction of a glossy, bland show home. But when Kristian bought it he made some wise decisions that brought warmth, texture and soul to the shiny remodelled space.

With a bit of guidance from his friends at Jersey Ice Cream Co. (who, despite their name, design homes rather than making ice cream), the home was given a vital injection of soul in the form of the painted shiplap timber used on the living-room walls, the lath on the side of the ground floor staircase and the reclaimed barn wood on the ceiling of the top-floor den. Adding wood of almost any kind to bare walls can have a huge impact for a relatively small outlay. Another trick Kristian employed was to add a fireplace to the living room to replace one that had been ripped out by the previous owner. Even though this one,

CREATIVITY BEFORE CONSUMPTION
Kristian came up with a slick idea for custom handles for his kitchen cabinets (above). He bought lengths of blank leather belting, cut it into strips and secured each one to the cabinet door with brass screws from the hardware store — a much less expensive (and much more gratifying) version of a store-bought equivalent. Belt blanks are available online.

Earth tones. Despite having quite a lot out on display, Kristian's home doesn't feel cluttered, thanks in part to his palette of woods, metals and natural tones. The dining area is between the kitchen and living room on the ground floor and has an antique bench and black Eames chairs around a contemporary wooden table (below). In the kitchen, copper pots and pans are hung from a long metal bar that runs along one wall and crosses a small window (opposite far left), patterned bowls and plates are stacked on shelves (opposite below right) and kitchen utensils are stored in a large ceramic pot found at an antiques market (opposite centre).

Every home should have...

One area devoted purely to relaxation – just comfortable furniture and plenty of cushions, with technology out of sight. Here, a sofa is covered in sheepskins and cushions sourced on a buying trip to Vietnam.

found at a flea market, doesn't function, it creates a central hub around which a group of chairs can gather.

When it comes to decorating, Kristian must have one of the best contact lists in the business and this came in handy when he wanted to find a few special pieces for his new home. The Chieftain chair by Finn Juhl was a house-warming present to himself, purchased with the help of the Danish company OneCollection. The old leather club chair was sourced for him in Paris by old friend and designer Steve Harivel and represents something of a shift in style from Kristian's collection of mostly Danish chairs, which he's been collecting since college. But he's just as likely to find something on Craigslist, such as his Chesterfield sofa, or on the street or at a yard sale, like his drafting table-turned-bar cart.

Mixed in with the vintage designer pieces and the street finds are objects chosen for the imprint of the artist's hand. As the child of a painter (and a senior buyer at a company that prides itself on artistry and originality), Kristian is drawn to handmade pieces. The shibori-dyed curtains in his guest bedroom are flat-woven dhurrie rugs, hand-dyed at a workshop in India, while the huge denim folk art flag above his bed was found at a junk shop and is beautifully stitched by hand.

Kristian's job as a buyer means that he's on the road for much of the year. As a result of all this travel, his home has a gorgeously eclectic style, filled with things he saw and loved and lugged home in his suitcase. It doesn't feel overly thought out, and it all works beautifully together. Kristian admits to being unable to resist buying pieces he sees on his travels, often putting up with the impracticality of getting them home because he knows that if he loves an item, it will work. For this buyer extraordinaire, the only things he ever regrets are the pieces he didn't buy.

Mid-century mood. In Kristian's bedroom, he has created a small seating area by the window, teaming a cosy armchair with a reading lamp. The dresser/hutch was a family piece, and while it looks like two different pieces of furniture stacked on top of each other, it is in fact one item. You could recreate this effect by pairing up two odd units and securing them with brackets at the back.

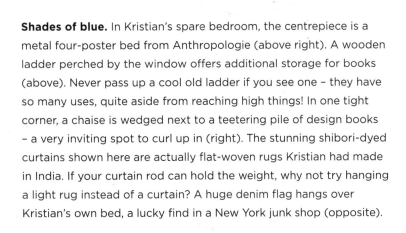

Shades of blue. In Kristian's spare bedroom, the centrepiece is a metal four-poster bed from Anthropologie (above right). A wooden ladder perched by the window offers additional storage for books (above). Never pass up a cool old ladder if you see one – they have so many uses, quite aside from reaching high things! In one tight corner, a chaise is wedged next to a teetering pile of design books – a very inviting spot to curl up in (right). The stunning shibori-dyed curtains shown here are actually flat-woven rugs Kristian had made in India. If your curtain rod can hold the weight, why not try hanging a light rug instead of a curtain? A huge denim flag hangs over Kristian's own bed, a lucky find in a New York junk shop (opposite).

A COLOURFUL *Collection*

Painterly touch. The kitchen was built by Dan as a temporary fix when they moved in years ago, but the chalky blue cupboards and white metro tiles are still going strong (above). The kitchen table was painted blue and découpaged on top (opposite). In the hallway, small antlers make quirky key-holders (above left).

DAN AND SARA DUCHARS NEVER INTENDED TO STAY IN THIS HOUSE FOR LONG. The plan was to fix it up, sell it on and buy their dream home. Instead, they ended up falling in love with the Victorian terraced house in East London's Clapton, and now, some 15 years later, share it with their two children, Alfred, aged 13, and Flossie, 11, and a lively collection of animals. Dan is an interiors and lifestyle photographer and Sara runs Button Bag, a craft company that creates kits for children and adults. Their charming home is a perfect expression of their gutsy creative style.

Like many of London's popular neighbourhoods, Clapton was once a very different place. When Dan and Sara moved in, there was not much more on offer than betting shops, discount stores and gang violence. Nowadays, nearby Chatsworth Road boasts an artisan deli and wine shop, vintage boutiques and independent shops and cafes mixed in with the long-standing retailers, as well as

On display. The stairway wall is home to an ever-growing gallery of framed family photos (far left), while a cabinet in the living room holds a vintage clock collection (left). Vases of dried flowers fill the living room mantelpiece (below), and rich hues of paint and textiles infuse the room with warmth (opposite). Rather than a large coffee table, a pair of leather pouffes make for a much more flexible arrangement. Printed cushions by Clarissa Hulse fill the sofa and chairs.

the once-defunct but recently reopened Sunday street market. Yes, it's been gentrified, but Clapton has managed to retain the soul of a proper British high street; a rare thing today when most towns share the same line-up of multinational retailers.

The Duchars' home is tucked away on a quiet side street. London is filled with streets like this – sweet little homes all in a row, most of them with identical floorplans. In fact my own house, not far from theirs, has the very same layout on the ground floor; a fact that made it all the more interesting to find out how they had made theirs unique.

I work with Dan on occasion, so the nosy part of me was curious about his home when I began researching this book. I suspected he and Sara would have an interesting place, based purely on the fact that I've seen him arrive on set in plaid trousers and stripy socks. He's obviously not going to live in a white box! Sara is equally stylish – think pink faux fur jackets and vintage embroidered skirts – so I had a hunch that their house would be stylish too. It certainly didn't disappoint, although I didn't have them pegged for taxidermy collectors!

This is a real family home, filled with bold colour choices, intriguing collections and tons of personality. It's a home that is unapologetically eclectic, an authentic look

Every home should have...

An area just for a prized collection. In this house there are many, including this one in the corner of the living room – the family's 'nature table' for rocks, shells and other objects picked up on walks over the years.

that has been built up over the years, with pieces being added and taken away as lifestyles and tastes change. Collections are a dominant theme – a rock collection on a shelf welcomes you immediately upon entering through the front door. In the living room, joining the stuffed badger and fox (found at a Belgian flea market and carried home on the back seat of the car in between the kids), are groups of vintage clocks and bird skulls, and on the 'nature table' a collection of interesting objects picked up on walks over the years. In Flossie's room, it's clear that she has inherited the collecting bug and that she really loves pigs. There are pig lights, crocheted pigs, flying pigs and pictures of pigs on roller skates, their pink hue clashing fantastically with Flossie's mustard walls.

The walls of this house are boldly painted in every room. There's a warm grey-brown shade in the hallway, a rich wine in the living room, chalky pale blue in the kitchen and deepest petrol blue in the master bedroom. I especially love the kids' colours: mustard and blue for Flossie (with pops of piggy pink, of course) and blue and lime green for Alfred, especially brave when combined with his glossy red cabinets. Not content with painting just the walls, each room's window and door frames have been coated in contrasting colours, adding another layer of interest to this characterful home.

In the kitchen, the couple carried out what was intended to be a quick-fix renovation, adding metro tiles, wooden cabinets painted in a distressed blue with antique handles and butcher-block worksurfaces. Many years later, the 'makeshift' kitchen is still going strong, proving that you don't need to spend a fortune on a kitchen for it to have style or to function well. Open shelving for pots and pans adds character, and family mementoes taped to walls

or perched on windowsills make this room feel like a loved and well-used space. A pair of wooden crates stacked in the corner serves a dual purpose – cookbook storage and family gadget charging station, a place to corral phones and tablets and all their wires and plugs. Every home needs one!

There's so much to take away from the Duchars' London home: be daring with colour, let your kids participate in the decorating process and proudly display whatever brings you joy. It's a home where everyone's needs are met and each family member's decorating style is represented; a true family home.

Boutique at home. In the master bedroom, there are whitewashed floorboards, petrol blue walls and a rich red and blue antique rug. Lack of adequate wardrobe/closet space means that Sara has a rolling clothes rack in the corner. Luckily her eclectic taste in clothes results in the bedroom looking like a cool vintage store. Adding to the charm is a tailor's bust, decked out in hats and belts (above).

Pretty organized. In Flossie's bedroom, a bold mustard theme was chosen for the walls, metal bedframe and bed linen. Blue Shaker-style pegboard shelves wrap around the walls. When painted a colour of your choice, these rails are really practical for kids' rooms, offering plenty of hanging space for all the small items they amass and want to display. Another idea to steal is the vintage plan chest by the bed, its many small drawers the perfect solution for keeping organized: one for drawings, one for hairclips, one for nail polish, one for pencils and so on (left).

CREATIVITY BEFORE CONSUMPTION
In Alfie's bedroom, a stack of glossy red IKEA cabinets is an unconventional choice that works as clothes storage, a room divider and a bedside table all in one (below left and right). Throw out the rule book about certain furniture only being suitable for certain rooms and suit yourself instead.

Creative corner. On the other side of Flossie's room, the wallpapered chimneybreast and a pair of small disco balls add a touch of glamour. Above her electric organ (which fits snugly in the nook), shelves were added to accommodate her books. Non-working fireplaces are pretty to look at, but often people struggle to know how to fill them. Here, a wooden trunk sits in front and holds extra clothes, while the mantelshelf is decorated with colourful pots (left).

103

Family ATELIER

THE BUILDING IN BRUSSELS that Eugenie Collet and Olivier Rouxhet call home has been in Eugenie's family since the late 19th century, and was in use as an art studio up until the early 1980s. Eugenie's great-grandfather built this workshop in 1895 for his decorative arts business, Les Etablissements Collet, specializing in high-level painting for interiors and exteriors as well as faux bois, faux marble and trompe l'œil. Now, the spacious, light-filled interior is home to Eugenie, Olivier and their children, Jeanne, aged 20, and Georges, 18.

Eugenie works as a production designer and set decorator for film, TV and advertising, while Olivier is a graphic designer. Fittingly, their home has a slightly theatrical mood; the numerous original glazed partition walls that once divided the atelier up into smaller workrooms and offices have been preserved throughout, and the space is also peppered with more graphic and modern additions.

Room within a room. In this former painting atelier, all the original glass-fronted cabinets remain in what is now the kitchen (above). When more storage was added in the hallway, rather than try to match the original woodwork, contemporary black-stained ply was chosen (above right). The family's sitting room was once an office within the atelier (opposite). This glass enclosure off the kitchen is small and cosy, with ebony-stained floors, a wood-burning stove and dark vintage furniture.

CREATIVITY BEFORE CONSUMPTION
The family has perfected the art of high–low decorating in their sitting room. Vintage lighting and furniture are an elegant addition, but it is the hand-painted IKEA lampshade that adds quirkiness. Inexpensive paper lampshades are easy to paint when opened up.

Homework. In a corner of the sitting room is a small desk for writing emails and doing family paperwork (opposite). It's also where they keep many of their books and collections of art and trinkets. Next to their desk is a pair of petite vintage armchairs where they often sit and read or where Eugenie works on her hand-sewn projects, like the embroidered cushions seen here (this page).

The kitchen is a light-drenched space, with a pitched ceiling made entirely of glass and walls lined from floor to ceiling with original cupboards and drawers. In its decorating studio heyday, Eugenie's great-grandfather's employees used this space to store paint cans and to mix the pigments with linseed oil. Luckily for Olivier and Eugenie, the abundance of cupboards and shelves provides plenty of room for their crockery and kitchenware as well as their many collections of ceramics and bric-a-brac, collected over the years at flea markets and displayed in a pleasingly haphazard fashion.

What attracts me to this home is the fact that almost everything is out on display. Eugenie and Olivier could have added cupboards to hide all their stuff, but they've chosen to keep it all on show, as if to say 'This is what we love, and this is who we are'. The walls of every room,

with the exception of the master bedroom, are crowded with artworks, many of them created by Eugenie herself. There is inspiration at every turn, from the collage of magazine tearsheets in Jeanne's room to the collection of framed art, collectibles and odds and ends on the wall behind Eugenie's desk. This is a visual family that likes to surround itself with inspiring imagery to stimulate the senses and kindle new ideas.

Eugenie and Olivier both work in the sunny, blue-floored studio. This mid-century addition to the building was once used as an office for the directors and secretaries of Les Etablissements Collet. It's here that Eugenie researches upcoming projects as well as creating her beautiful hand-stitched art, a side project and labour of love quite separate to her work as a set decorator. The floors in this room are made from old linoleum sheeting

Storage envy. Very little has changed here since the days when Eugenie's great-grandfather built this as his painting/decorating atelier. Shelves that once held pots of paint and brushes now contain the family's many collections of crockery and ceramics, and their kitchenware (above left). The glass-fronted cupboards reveal the mismatched collections and it feels refreshingly honest – a functional, working kitchen blessed with natural light from the glass roof (opposite). Paint finishes on the cupboards were left rough and unfinished (above), and there is nothing flashy here, except perhaps the stainless steel oven and fridge (left).

Simply grand. Eugenie and Olivier's bedroom is big, with very grand windows. It's reached via some stairs and a trap door, and feels quite separate from the rest of the house. Despite its size they have kept things simple, with a handsome platform bed, a towering bookshelf and a long bench (below). The embroidered bedding was hand-sewn by Eugenie (opposite). Within the room is yet another room, enclosed with glass. As an atelier it had been an area for painting large items like pianos. Now it is the master bathroom, decorated simply with chequerboard floor tiles and a cast-iron bathtub (left).

painted an invigorating shade of aqua, and a long cream curtain divides the space. Behind this curtain is a guest bedroom, one wall lined with books for visitors, and a projector that's set up for family movie watching.

In 2011, a large garage at the front of the building was converted into two bedrooms for the children. On a slightly raised level and accessed by wooden stairs, the rooms are small but stylish, with loft-style beds and windows to let in light. I've always been a fan of making it up as you go along, and for me this applies to homes as much as anything else. Some people want everything to be 'perfect' right away, but Eugenie and Olivier are happy to tweak things as they go along, adding rooms or changing their purpose as the family's needs change.

What strikes me most about this extraordinary home is the care that has been taken to maintain the integrity of the original building, while also breathing new life into it as a family home and creative hub. It's rare for a building to remain within a family for generations, and rarer still for a current owner to faithfully perserve the original spirit of the space, but Eugenie and Olivier have done just that.

A place for kids to experiment with their style. This fun space (below) is painted white so that the mood-board wall can speak for itself. Let kids use magazine pages, postcards and drawings to express themselves.

Double duty. An extension was added in the 1950s as an office for the atelier's directors. Now the long room is divided into work areas for the couple (above), and at the far end, behind a white curtain, is a guest bedroom (opposite). In the guest room there is a wall of media and a projector to watch films. The floors are old linoleum that the couple painted blue, an uplifting choice for a room where ideas and creativity need to happen. Painting over linoleum is a good option when an inexpensive quick fix is required.

Natural styling. Despite its small size, a huge amount of personality has been packed into the living room (opposite). Shelves flank the chimneybreast and another was added above the non-working fireplace to provide more surface space for this globe-trotting couple's collections, largely picked up on their travels (above left). Potted plants and vases of branches bring the room to life and last longer than cut flowers (above).

Brixton
BIJOU

YOU'D NEVER GUESS, BUT A MERE FIVE MINUTES' WALK from this tranquil apartment is bustling Brixton Village, one of South London's most vibrant areas. For six years now, Stephanie Zak and Ben Johnson have called this bijou flat their home, creating a stylish and calm haven in the centre of town. When Stephanie bought the flat – it was her first home – it was an an unfinished shell and over the years she has transformed it into the cosy retreat it is today. A photographic shoot producer working mostly in interiors, she has clearly picked up a few pointers along the way and found the perfect balance between a styled and natural look. Ben is a music producer who often works from home, so it's important that the flat is calming and inspiring, both of which are true.

Line the walls. Open shelving in both the living room and kitchen allows the couple's style to shine through. The fireplace shelves display decorative items like small plants, pictures and books, while the cupboards beneath serve as a drinks cabinet and storage for extra glassware, candles, vases and other things they'd rather not have on show (above). In the small galley kitchen just off the living room, storage is limited (opposite). Shelves are organized into cookbooks, pots/pans, dinnerware and glassware. A large framed poster hangs on the wall, adding further to the personality of the home.

Located one flight up in a 1930s red-brick block, the flat is petite – one small bedroom, an open-plan living room with a galley kitchen and a bathroom. The couple have added storage wherever possible: there are built-in units in the living room, a large mirrored wardrobe in the bedroom and stacks of vintage suitcases filled to the brim.

Home and travel are priorities for Stephanie and Ben, who have found a way to combine their two passions. They rent out the flat to other travellers and the additional income they earn allows them to feed their insatiable desire to travel. Playing host has encouraged them to create order in their small home without sacrificing style. On display are cherished mementoes – photos, art and small collections – but care has also been taken to make it a well-functioning space so guests can find what they need.

The flat is decorated with a charming mix of vintage finds, furniture found on the street and then refurbished, and accessories collected on their travels. The Moroccan wedding blanket on their bed was found in a souk in Marrakech and was a birthday gift from Ben to Stephanie, while the turquoise sari repurposed as bedroom curtains was picked up in Malaysia. Also thrown into the mix is artwork inherited from Stephanie's Swiss grandparents and sculptures made by her sculptor mother. All in all, it makes for an enchanting home, the kind of place that compels you to stop and take it all in.

I imagine you learn to be relaxed when you allow strangers to rent your home. You have little choice but to be chilled out about the fact that people are going to touch your stuff! And it shows in the sweetly laid-back way that Stephanie has styled, or rather not styled, her things. I particularly love the shelves flanking the fireplace, where all manner of odds and ends jostle for space – photobooth snaps, dried flowers and branches, candles and postcards. It feels special but not too precious and it feels alive, as if it's constantly evolving, thanks to the inspiration that the couple bring back from each trip.

CREATIVITY BEFORE CONSUMPTION
The small bedroom features some great ideas.
Curtains made from a sari add colour and filter
light beautifully; a suitcase makes a bedside
table for the tight space; and a wooden hanger
is a creative way to display paper tassels.

Maximize your space. In the small bedroom, every inch of space is put to good use (opposite). The windowsill is lined with small plants and gilt frames (above left) and a very tight nook at the foot of the bed gets a wooden side table for dishes of jewellery and vases of flowers, with a dressmaker's bust adding character and doubling as necklace storage (left). To make up for the lack of built-in storage, Stephanie collects vintage suitcases and stacks them along the wall to hold items that she doesn't need to access frequently, such as off-season clothes (above).

Warehouse
TREASURE TROVE

JUST MOMENTS FROM THE BUSY ANGEL INTERSECTION in North London stands this converted commercial building, the private retreat of an art collector, artist and writer. Tucked away discreetly in a gated mews, it was once a graphic design studio, but with the help of 6a Architects and the homeowner's exquisite taste, the building has been converted into a multi-layered, light-filled home.

If you stumbled upon the building, you probably wouldn't give it a second glance – a fact that no doubt pleases the very private homeowner. That's not to say the 1950s concrete lintel and steel frame warehouse doesn't have its merits, but it looks much like any other commercial building in central London, its exterior not hinting at what lies within. There is nothing ostentatious about it, and with its mysterious reeded glass windows on the ground-floor level, you'd be forgiven for thinking the only things inside were ancient printing presses gathering dust. But this is not the case. Inside the unassuming brick and concrete exterior are 345 square metres/3,700 square feet of beauty, creativity and inspiration; a feast for the senses.

When it comes to warehouse living, there seems to be two stereotypes: firstly, the masculine, over-designed look of the bachelor with cash to spend – a Harley Davidson in the living room and a Porsche in the garage – and then there's the 12-creatives-sharing-a-warehouse-in-a-dodgy-part-of-town look.

Texture and tone. This warehouse conversion's neutral palette allows for a dizzying array of art, textiles and collections to be layered throughout. Art is tucked in the rafters, collections gather on tables and the line between what is art and what is not is blurred (right).

A few baskets dotted around to catch the day-to-day build-up of life's stuff. Keep one by the stairs to collect bits that need to go up and one in the living room for throws when it gets chilly.

Art life. In the kitchen of this art collector, there is so much more on display than the usual kitchen gadgets (above). A shelf that runs the length of the wall is loaded with items gathered over the years: antique pharmacy bottles, a black matryoshka doll from Muji, a jug by Nicola Tassie and vases by Akiko Hirai, some with floral cuttings casually tucked in (right). Even the splashback is an opportunity to indulge in some art, with tiles by artist Paula Rego.

Archive at home. An unusual but endlessly practical choice, these metal archive cabinets roll along one side of the space and contain clothing and accessories on the bedroom end, books and ceramic collections near the middle and crockery and dry goods near the kitchen (above). Even the ends are put to good use as an ever-changing moodboard for postcards, invitations, tearsheets and photos.

This one has mattresses on shipping pallets and bicycles hung on the walls. There's nothing wrong with either scenario, but how exciting it is to find a place that mixes high-spec design with bohemian creativity.

What's most striking about this home is the sheer quantity of art it contains – paintings, sculptures and ceramics – and the nonchalance with which the art is displayed. Together the homeowner and architect have designed a perfect blank canvas upon which to layer her collection of art. For some, the abundance of 'stuff' might be too much, but what prevents this space from feeling cluttered is the beautiful, simple backdrop and the way

everything is linked by a palette of natural materials and colours. Yet, despite its free-spirited style, the attention to detail here is anything but laid-back. There's underfloor heating, remote-controlled blinds, museum-quality UV glass to protect the artwork, a state-of-the-art security system and archive storage units on floor runners.

The expansive home is set over two floors with a spiral staircase leading from the kitchen to a roof garden. The ground floor is home to two large art studios, not shown here. The first floor comprises the entire living area, a 26-metre/86-foot-long rectangular space divided up into distinct kitchen/dining, living, sleeping and bathing areas

Creative chaos. The natural elements of the living room create an earthy, snug haven. Layers of soft rugs and cushions beckon from the sofa, while hand-made textiles created by the owner hang from bars, dividing the open-plan space. Framed art is casually lined up on skinny shelves.

Layered life. Tucked at the far end of the space is the bedroom (opposite), separated from the main living area by a curtain, which creates a calm and private oasis for rest and relaxation. Also helping to separate the bedroom from the rest of the living space is a group of potted plants surrounding a chaise (left). Piles of throws and a group of small animal-skin rugs grouped tightly on the floor make a potentially cold environment a cocoon of warmth and comfort. Above the bed is a skinny shelf with art and photography propped casually along it (below). A bookshelf beneath the window provides another display surface as well as useful storage (below left).

by the strategic positioning of curtains, furniture and plants. The floors are polished concrete, the walls are mostly white and the furniture is an interesting mix of vintage Scandinavian pieces.

For me, the most impressive feature is the use of museum storage cabinets. These are a nod to the owner's past life as a curator as well as an archive of her belongings. Each unit is beautifully organized: those close to the kitchen hold crockery and food, those near the living area are packed with books and units by the bedroom are filled with clothes, shoes and accessories. With one turn of the handle, the huge metal units glide open on their runners, instantly transforming the layout of the open-plan space.

The homeowner's involvement in the art world is evident everywhere. In fact, there is little here that isn't a work of art, from the tiles in the kitchen to the huge

bird's nest tucked up in the rafters and the barely visible spray of paint on some of the walls. Often in homes where art plays a starring role things can feel static, like a museum where everything is kept behind ropes. But in this treasure trove of a home the owner has managed to create a space that feels both artistic and accessible, an autobiographical installation where every piece is infused with meaning; either a memory of her past or maybe a wish for the future.

We may not all have the funds to collect art or convert a warehouse to such exacting standards, but this home shows how to live with things you love in a way that is neither precious nor contrived. Life Unstyled means many things: creativity, authenticity, creating your own rules. But mostly it means allowing your home to be a true reflection of who you are at any given moment in time, and this is precisely what the owner has done here.

Casual elegance. Also at the
far end of the loft, opposite the
bed, is a small and simple desk
and chair, decorated simply with
more framed art and small vases
(right). Throughout the loft there
are so many pieces of art, yet
nothing feels precious. Much of
the art is hung – often at unusual
heights, high or low – but some of
it is simply propped on surfaces.
Opposite the bed, next to the
bathtub, a pair of tiny wooden
stools holds bath soap and
flowers, showing how it pays
to break the rules when it comes
to unconventional furniture
(above and opposite).

CREATIVITY BEFORE CONSUMPTION

An old bathtub was rescued and re-enamelled on the inside and upper exterior only, leaving the outside mostly rough. Rather than placing the tub on traditional decorative feet, a stack of bricks was used. Various hanging sculptures add to this unconventional bathroom.

At home WITH NATURE

LOU AND GAVIN ROTA HAVE LIVED IN North West London for more than 15 years, adapting their Edwardian semi-detached house as their family has grown. Through years of travel, collecting and re-inventing, the couple has created a unique, personal space to share with their daughters, Rosie, 16, and Ava, 14.

Lou and Gavin met years ago when they both worked in TV – Gavin is director of development for a production company, and Lou used to produce science and natural history programmes. However, about 11 years ago, she decided to go back to her roots as a designer and began upcycling old furniture, adding découpage and transfers to give new life to old pieces. This was before upcycling became popular, and Lou caught the eye of the buyers at Liberty at just the right time, going on to customize furniture for the iconic London store.

New York in London. At the back of the house is the recently added kitchen/dining/general hanging-out space, where exposed brickwork and beams lend an industrial New York loft vibe (opposite and above left). But the way the Rotas have chosen to decorate is far from industrial, with a mixture of antiques, upcycled street finds, and pieces bought at prop houses filling the space. The dining table is surrounded by chairs from an old church and is lit with bare bulbs (above right).

Soon after, Lou began buying vintage plates from antique markets and junk shops and adding her own water-slide transfer images of animals and insects. These were picked up by buyers at Liberty and Selfridges, and soon she was making a name for herself with her whimsical designs featuring birds and animals interacting with vintage florals on plates and other china. Soon after, Lou came to the attention of the buyers for Anthropologie, with whom she ended up collaborating on what is now a very successful line of vintage-inspired plates adorned with unexpected animal motifs – giraffes, praying mantis and blowfish are a few of my favourites.

Lou's dedication to creating something fresh and new from what was tired and old is also evident in her home. Aside from the beds, a few lights, and the kitchen, the entire house has been decorated with items sourced at antiques markets, junk shops and eBay; a great source of satisfaction for the couple, who strive for authenticity and sustainability.

Potted. Baby cacti nestle inside a large vintage bowl (above). If you line the base with gravel to allow for drainage, any interesting vessel can become a plant pot.

A cabinet or even a shelf for those special bits of glassware and china that you just can't help collecting. Lou had one built from salvaged wood, backing it with mirror glass to reflect light and make it seem deeper.

Contrasts. A wall in the reception room is papered in a stunning mural wallpaper by artist Jessica Zoob for Romo Black Edition (opposite and above right). In front of that is the sofa, re-upholstered in a variety of floral fabrics and at the far end of the room, floor-to-ceiling bookcases are painted in the startlingly bright Pantone Process Blue, a brilliant contrast to all the femininity (above left).

In the living room at the front of the house, a second-hand sofa has been recovered in a mismatched collection of muted floral fabrics, a gentle contrast to the floor to ceiling bookshelves at the other end, which have been painted in bold Pantone Process Blue. Upstairs, in their shared home office, Gavin and Lou's desk was constructed from a long wooden worktop with old banisters for legs and a worn set of drawers with iron knobs and pulls. In one of the girl's rooms, a collection of eBay-sourced drawer pulls was added to a black-painted dresser that now boasts no less than 15 mismatched handles.

Everything here seems to have a story. Even in the new kitchen – now double its original size, thanks to an addition last year – the couple have managed to create a sense of history. Exposed brick and beams, old wooden dining furniture, vintage shelf brackets and reclaimed wood and mirrored units work together to soften the effect of the fresh white kitchen cabinets and shiny new tiles.

The Rota family's love of the arts and culture, of science and nature is evident here. Their preference for pieces with history and patina over anything brand new makes for a home that's bursting with brilliant ideas to take away. It is also a valuable reminder that old doesn't have to mean old-fashioned – a stylish home filled with upcycled pieces and layered with family history can be the height of modernity and originality.

Away from it all. At the end of the garden is Lou's studio, a small, calm space among the trees (below left). Her desk faces the window, where she tapes up inspiration or illustrations in progress. The shelves are filled with stacks of vintage plates and cups – the inspiration for her collections (left and far left). She buys them at antiques markets and adds her own designs to the vintage florals, giving them a modern whimsical edge. One of her plate designs, illustrated by hand, hangs below miniature magnets of her past designs (below).

CREATIVITY BEFORE CONSUMPTION

In the shared office space the desk is made from a long piece of salvaged wood atop a slightly battered cabinet and chunky banisters. The drawer pulls have been replaced with some sourced on eBay and arranged from small to big, an eye-catching and thoughtful detail. Vintage metal shelf brackets were also sourced online.

Feminine touch. On the top floor, in Ava's room, a black-and-white floral wallpaper helps to create an environment that is feminine but still modern and young (left). In the master bedroom, a beautiful old chair sits next to a patchwork curtain, now about 30 years old (above). The curtain was originally from their former home and had been left behind by the previous owner. Lou hired a seamstress to patch up the worn areas with fabric scraps.

Blackout. In the master bedroom, Lou wanted to paint the whole room dark. Gavin wasn't so sure, so a compromise was made with the dark bookcases and chimneybreast (left). In Rosie's room, the dark theme continues with her bedding, punctuated by bright oversized cushions she made for a school project (below). Her dresser also got a coat of black paint and its fifteen drawers each got a 'new but old' metal pull (below left). Lou swears by eBay for doorknobs, drawer pulls and shelf brackets and has updated most of her drawers and dressers in this way.

Minimalist
WITH A TWIST

YOLANDA CHIARAMELLO AND JAMES WATERS are friends of mine. Yolanda (Yolly to her friends) and I have known each other since we were 15. We lost touch when I moved to the States but reconnected thanks to good old social media. One of the many joys of being back in London is our renewed friendship, and it's been such a pleasure to meet her sweet family and watch them grow.

Yolly is a florist and photographer, James a producer, and home for them is a light-filled sixth-floor flat in South East London that they share with their boys, Enzo and Jacob, aged six and nine. The family had been living in the area for five years before they bought this three-bedroom flat in a 1960s housing development called Dulwich Estates. Development in the area began in the late 1950s, bringing a sense of community to this wooded parkland close to central London, and from the stories I hear from James and Yolly, that community still thrives today. It's an idyllic setting for raising a young family – many of the children on the estate go to the same schools, while their parents socialize together and help each other out if someone can't make the school run in time. There is a sense of neighbourly care, concern and friendship.

Yolly and James's flat is a great example of city living done right. With London property prices the way they are (i.e. prohibitively high), often a flat is the only way to get on the property ladder. In order to buy in a neighbourhood they

Modern eclectic. With an excellent eye for furniture placement, this couple have carved multiple areas from one room (right). The sofa was given by a neighbour, the table from an old pub, the chairs from a school and the rug from a street market in Kiev.

own apartments as well, creating little time warps tucked away behind closed doors. Yolly and James had different ideas, creating instead a home that blends modern with vintage and minimalist with quirky.

When they bought the flat in late 2014, it was horribly out of date and a million style miles away from the airy space seen on these pages. The couple set to work gutting the place and doing what they could in the weeks before they had to vacate their rented flat and move in. Carpets were ripped up, strangely placed doors removed and the kitchen was completely torn out and redesigned with the help of friend, neighbour and carpenter Dave Cowling.

The renovations continued after they moved in and there's still work to be done. The bathroom and kitchen are finished; layers of paint on the Crittall windows have been scraped off to reveal the original steel frames; bedroom floors have been painted; one wall has been refinished in a stunning chalky pink Venetian plaster. Next on the list is repairing and refinishing the hardwood floors, adding more storage, building bunk beds for the boys and replacing the front door.

Despite this long to-do list, the flat feels incredibly welcoming. It exudes a simple, chic style and strikes a fine balance between raw and refined and modern and vintage. Yolly and James don't have much furniture, but everything they do own has character, a history or has been made by hand. Their home doesn't feel cluttered, but neither does it feel cold in the way some more minimalist homes can do. The couple's collection of vintage furniture and lighting plays off the modernist lines of the flat. Add to that mix newly built cabinets, shelves and benches in stained and painted birch ply and the look is modern, youthful and unique – just like my friends.

had grown to love, Yolly and James had to make compromises, giving up on a garden and a second bathroom. But as their sons are still young and the flat offers easy access to nearby Dulwich Woods, both were things that they decided they could live without.

The common areas of the building retain many of their original mid-century features, such as the foyer clad in retro tiles and wood panelling, doors painted bright orange and beautiful Crittall windows throughout. Some of the building's residents favour a mid-century style for their

Calm corner. Because their boys share a room, the third bedroom can be used for guests and as a quiet space for reading or working at home (above). A sofa bed, a vintage desk and chair and another rug from Kiev are all that is needed in this calm space. An old leather suitcase is used as a coffee table, and is filled with Yolly's vintage shoe collection.

Every home should have...

An easy-to-reach spot for kids to stash their homework and art supplies. Here, shelves were built into the outside of the kitchen counters to catch the overflow from the kitchen, including candles, napkins and tablecloths.

Vintage modern mix. A large industrial metal shelving unit sits against a wall in the flat's entrance and has plenty of room for shoes, rucksacks and sports equipment (below). Look out for these at antiques markets – they can be used in any room to store almost anything. In the bathroom, birch plywood is again used for a minimalist but warm finish (below left). The small enamel sink is from Labour and Wait and is just the thing for a bathroom this size. The taps/faucets were custom-made with basic plumbing supplies and copper piping.

CREATIVITY BEFORE CONSUMPTION

Instead of a traditional bedside table in the master bedroom, a wooden crate has been painted yellow and turned on its side to store books (left). A chair is also used to hold a blue Jieldé lamp. The room is sparsely decorated, but the cheerful choice of paint colour and bedding prevent it looking cold.

Colour pop. Even though this is a three-bedroom flat, the boys share a room, an idea that helps to foster closeness between siblings – if you can put up with the occasional turf war (above). Their shared bedroom has shelves, cupboards and a desk custom-built with birch plywood, most of it getting a coat of blue or yellow paint (left).

Space to create. This jewellery designer has cobbled together a workspace with a variety of filing cabinets and antique drawers for the paraphernalia of her craft (opposite and above left). The dining table is surrounded by a mix of wood, leather and metal chairs, some of them found at a yard sale (above). An oversize IKEA light hangs above and the wall behind is covered in art by family and friends.

ART BY THE
Bridge

NOT TOO LONG AGO, GENEVIEVE HUDSON-PRICE AND STEFAN MAROLACHAKIS were each living in cramped apartments on Manhattan's Lower East Side. Three years on, home is a 185-square-metre/2000-square-foot loft in an 1894 landmarked building in Brooklyn's DUMBO district, formerly home to the *Brooklyn Eagle* newspaper. For Genevieve – an actress, jewellery designer and gallerist – being in the heart of the arts district is a source of constant inspiration. The Brooklyn Bridge looms large right outside their apartment window, an awe-inspiring view to wake up to. With Genevieve's involvement in the arts and Stefan's work as a musician and writer, the all-white open-plan space is somewhere they can spread out and pursue their interests.

CREATIVITY BEFORE CONSUMPTION

Rather than spend money on an extra-long dining table, the couple use two inexpensive plastic fold-out trestle tables, which they've covered with wax fabric and lit with a large paper pendant light from IKEA. This thrifty solution allows them flexibility depending on their needs, with each table able to fold flat and tuck away when not needed.

status prevents any enlargement or addition of windows. Then they filled it with art – by Genevieve's mother, Judith Hudson, by friends of the family and emerging artists Genevieve meets via her nomadic gallery 7Eleven, a collaboration with a property developer that allows her to use spaces that are in pre-development as a temporary exhibition space. The walls of the loft are covered in paintings, photography and sculptures, all arranged in a pleasingly haphazard fashion. Even some of the rugs and the wallpaper are artist-made, and the Rob Wynne butterfly wallpaper is given an extra-special twist by the installer mistakenly hanging it upside down.

The white-painted floors and walls in the large space allow for a vast array of colours and patterns to be added without things feeling out of control. There are textiles and art in yellow, blue, orange, pink and green, but carried through the home is a thread of rich red. It's a strong colour choice and, when mixed with eclectic prints and furniture, feels bold and modern.

Although there's more art here than you'd find in most homes, the loft manages to maintain a relaxed vibe rather than a stuffy 'look-but-don't-touch' feeling. You get the impression that things are moved around a lot and that it's all a work in progress. Nowhere is this more evident than in Genevieve's jewellery-making corner, an L-shaped space made up of a hotchpotch of tables and cabinets. Here, Genevieve sits, surrounded by tools and materials, hand-crafting an eclectic collection of one-of a-kind pieces for her business. Named Blue Morpho Jewelry after the butterfly of the same name, her pieces incorporate real butterfly wings, beetles and spider webs encased in hand-carved crystal and 14-carat gold. (Only dormant spider webs and insects that have died of natural causes are used.)

Genevieve grew up in the New York art world of the 1980s and '90s, her childhood home a revolving door of artist friends of her mother and father, a painter and novelist/screenwriter respectively. She was encouraged to create from a young age, her mother valuing creative exploration over high scores on maths tests.

When the couple moved in here three years ago, they did little more than paint everything white and add slivers of mirror to the windowsills to bounce more light into the apartment; a stroke of genius in a building whose landmark

Ships in the night. Inspired by the bank-breakingly expensive crystal chandeliers shaped like ships, Genevieve made her own budget-friendly version by hanging sailing ship kites on bare pendant lights in the entrance hallway (above left). Against the chocolate brown walls, the ghostly white ships float near the ceiling, an enchanting way to welcome guests to their home. The kites are by Brooklyn-based Haptic Lab.

Every home should have...

Plenty of throws and textiles to protect, soften and liven up your seating. A white fitted sheet on the sofa (below) and a length of blue plaid fabric on the armchair (right) are inexpensive, no-sew solutions for protecting furniture.

Creative thinking. The kitchen corner is small and basic but has been brought to life with lots of colourful collections out on display. The kitchen island was made from a metal workbench bought from a hardware store and topped with wood.

Brighten it up. Colour is introduced to the small bedroom with bright linen pillowcases and more of Genevieve's collection of Dutch wax fabric spread on the bed (above left). A shelf made from books shows off Genevieve's DIY skills. This cupboard came with the apartment and now sits between the two bedrooms, displaying more of the pair's treasures (above right).

Genevieve is an avid collector of trinkets, scouring New York's junk shops and flea markets for inspiring pieces that she can cast in silver or gold. Her work area is overflowing with collections of miniatures and precious stones waiting to be transformed into something magical.

Throughout the apartment the same relaxed attitude applies to the furniture. Simple white slipcovered sofas and armchairs are layered with throws, tapestries and pieces of fabric, adding pops of colour and protecting them from wear. A pendant light and a red cabinet from IKEA sit alongside a pair of Noguchi lamps and a vintage modernist chair. The dining table is made up of two inexpensive trestle tables covered up by yards of Dutch wax fabric, the edges left raw, and surrounded by chairs found at a yard sale. I suspect the couple would rather spend their money on a new piece of art than a proper dining table, and I love their resourcefulness.

In the kitchen, creative thinking is again in evidence, with a metal workbench from a hardware catalogue and topped with a butcher's block in use as an island. More than anything, it is this mix of utilitarian and beautiful and high and low that makes this home so original, in addition to the couple's devotion to the arts and their disregard of traditional interior-design rules.

SOURCE LIST

UK/EUROPE

Emily Henson, interior stylist and author.
Find me on Instagram, Pinterest, Twitter and Facebook @lifeunstyled
Blog: lifeunstyled.com
Styling portfolio: emilyhensonstudio.com

Abigail Ahern
137 Upper Street
London N1 1QP
+44 20 7354 8181
abigailahern.com
Furniture, lighting, accessories and a brilliant collection of faux flowers and plants.

Baileys Home
Whitecross Farm
Bridstow
Herefordshire HR9 6JU
+44 (0)1989 561931
baileyshome.com
Mark and Sally Bailey have put together the most incredible selection of vintage and vintage-inspired homewares – their wooden crates, hand forged nails, and copper S-hooks are staples in my styling kit.

Le BHV Marais
52 rue de Rivoli
Paris 75004
France
+33 9 77 40 14 00
www.bhv.fr
Head to the basement of this Parisian department store for the most comprehensive selection of hardware and DIY supplies I've ever seen in one place. When I set up Anthropologie's first Parisian store, it was a lifesaver.

Deborah Bowness
www.deborahbowness.com
My favourite wallpaper designer – hang one of her rolls from a bulldog clip and a sturdy nail for an instant wallhanging.

Camden Passage
Islington
London N1 8EA
Camdenpassageislington.co.uk
Interesting shops and antiques markets tucked away in the heart of Angel.

Caravan
Caravanstyle.com
A unique selection of homeware and gifts curated by stylist and author Emily Chalmers. Ceramic swans, vintage floral cushions and golden tape measures.

Cass Art
cassart.co.uk
Everything you need to start customizing your possessions or making your own art – papers, paints, brushes and craft supplies.

Cloth House
47 Berwick Street
London W1F 8SJ
+44 (0)20 7437 5155
clothhouse.com
Responsibly sourced cotton, linen and handmade fabrics from around the world. When I want to change my sofa I buy a couple of metres of handprinted fabric and make new throw cushions.

Earthborn Paints
www.earthbornpaints.co.uk
Environmentally-friendly paints. I especially like their Claypaint for an ultra-matt, almost chalky finish.

Abigail Edwards
www.abigailedwards.com
This talented British stylist and designer adds her own designs to wallpaper, fabrics and home accessories. I love her Seascape and Storm Clouds wallpapers.

Happy Piece
happypiece.com
Brightly coloured hand-woven baskets ethically produced by a small cooperative in Rwanda. A collection of these looks brilliant hung on a wall.

H&M
hm.com
Inexpensive and stylish range of textiles and small accessories for the home.

IKEA
ikea.com
Say what you will about this retail giant, but I find some good stuff here, particularly their designer collaborations. Also good for buying basics to personalize.

Little Greene
www.littlegreene.com
Nice selection of wallpapers and a huge variety of vibrant coloured floor paints.

Merci
111 Boulevard Beaumarchais
Paris 75003
France
+33 1 42 77 00 33
www.merci-merci.com
A trip to Paris wouldn't be complete without a visit to this homeware and fashion emporium. Brightly coloured linen pillowcases, Japanese kitchen gadgets and bodega wine glasses often find their way into my suitcase.

Molly Meg
111 Essex Road
London N1 2SL
+44 (0)20 7359 5655
www.mollymeg.com
Owner Molly Price curates a modern, quirky selection of children's furniture, accessories, toys, and décor in her fun London shop and online. This is my go-to shop when I'm styling a children's shoot – I love the wall stickers.

Montana Cans
www.montana-cans.com
A large selection of good quality spray paint colours for quick creative projects.

New Covent Garden Flower Market
Nine Elms
London SW8 5BH
www.newcoventgarden-market.com
This wholesale flower market is also open to the public and sells every flower, branch and plant imaginable, as well as floristry and potting supplies. Get there early before they start to shut up shop at 9am.

Retrouvius
1016 Harrow Road
London NW10 5NS
+44 20 8960 6060
www.retrouvius.com
If you can't make it to an antiques market, Retrouvius have a well-edited selection of vintage furniture, accessories, and architectural salvage both online and at their north London warehouse.

RG Scott's Furniture Mart
The Old Ice Works
Bath Place
Margate
Kent CT9 2BN
+44 1843 220653
scottsmargate.co.uk
The selfish part of me might regret sharing this gem. I grew up near Margate and used to go here with my mum. Secondhand everything, and cheap! Visit the newly refurbished Dreamland amusement park nearby, and then load up the car with chairs, mirrors, bird cages, metal letters....

Sunbury Antiques Market at Kempton
Kempton Park Racecourse
Staines Road East
Sunbury-on-Thames
TW16 5AQ
sunburyantiques.com
Not too far from Central London, this antiques market draws stallholders from France, Belgium, and the UK. Held on the second and last Tuesday of every month.

Surface View
www.surfaceview.co.uk
A dazzling selection of wallpapers, murals and window films custom made to your exact specifications.

USA

ABC Carpet & Home
www.abchome.com
Inspiration is everywhere you look at this beautiful homeware emporium, even if most of it is uber-expensive.

Anthropologie
www.anthropologie.com
Stores in both the US and the UK. An eclectic mix of everything from mugs to rugs to beds, with inspiring merchandising and handmade displays. (They also sell clothes, but for me it's all about the homeware).

Blick Art
www.dickblick.com
Everything you need to start customizing and making your own art, including papers, paints, brushes and craft supplies.

Brooklyn Flea
www.Brooklynflea.com
Flea markets operating in Fort Greene on Saturdays and DUMBO on Sundays.

Ebay
www.ebay.com
Still a great resource for bidding on vintage drawer pulls, decorative shelf brackets, and other small items useful for updating furniture.

Rose Bowl Flea Market
10001 Rose Bowl Drive
Pasadena
California 91103
www.rgcshows.com
Huge antiques and collectibles market held on the second Sunday of every month.

Society of St Vincent de Paul Thrift Store
210 N Ave 21
Los Angeles, CA 90031
This was my weekly haunt when I was a stylist in Los Angeles. Like most thrift stores, it's a bit hit or miss, but I scored some of my favourite things in this huge warehouse.

Stella Dallas Living
281 N 6th Street
Brooklyn, NY 11211
Debi Treloar took me here when we were shooting for this book and I still dream about it. Stacks of vintage textiles fill this space – faded floral curtains, lace, quilts, vintage fabric and wool blankets. I can't recommend it enough.

Michele Varian
27 Howard Street
New York, NY 10013
212 343 0033
www.michelevarian.com
Wallpapers, fabrics, accessories and lighting by independent designers.

Pearl River
pearlriver.com
So many Chinese things you never knew you needed – painted silk lanterns, bamboo blinds (for you to customize with paint, perhaps?) and hand towels printed with a wonky 'Good Morning'.

PICTURE CREDITS

BUSINESS CREDITS

Myriam Balaÿ
www.myriambalay.fr
Pages 4, 5 below right, 6-7, 24 below right, 32 above left, 37, 44-45, 48-57.

Martin Bourne
Stylist
Martin is represented by Jed Root LA, inc
www.jedroot.com
Pages 8-10, 22-23, 43 left, 76-85.

Ramdane Touhami and Victoire de Taillac-Touhami
www.buly1803.com
Pages 5 below left, 13, 19-21, 24 below left, 30-31, 32 above right, 66-75.

Yolanda Chiaramello
Photography and floral design
www.chiaramello.co.uk
James Waters
Producer
www.choppywaters.com
Venetian-style plastering by Christian Chiaramello
Specialist Plasterer
cchiaramello@yahoo.co.uk
and
orange wool cushion covers from That's Well Lush
www.facebook.com/thatswelllush/
Pages 12 above left, 25 below left, 28 above, 33, 43 right, 140-145.

David Cowling
www.davidcowling.org
Pages 25 above left, 28 below, 36 above right, 40 right, 41, 42.

Sara and Dan Duchars
Sara Duchars
www.buttonbag.co.uk
Dan Duchars
T: +44 (0)7976 750 827
E: dan@danduchars.com
www.danduchars.com
Pages 12 above right, 14, 16 below left, 18 above right, 18 below, 36 above left, 96-103.

Eugénie Collet
https://www.facebook.com/Eugenie.Florence
Pages 1-3, 15, 18 above left, 26-27, 29, 36 below right, 104-113.

Genevieve Hudson-Price
Blue Morpho Jewelry
E: info@bluemorphojewelry.com
www.bluemorphojewelry.com
Endpapers, pages 11 left, 46-47, 146-53.

Sybil Domond and Daniel Lessin
People of 2morrow
65 Franklyn Street
Brooklyn
NY 11222
USA
www.peopleof2morrow.com
Pages 24 above left, 32 below right, 40 left, 58-65.

Lou Rota
www.lourota.com
Location to hire
lourota@icloud.com
T: + 44 (0)7941 357981
Pages 35 below, 130-139, 160.

Stephanie Zak's home is available to rent via Airbnb
https://www.airbnb.co.uk/rooms/797551?s=CyjQtqOP
Pages 11 right, 16, 17 right, 114-119, 155.

ACKNOWLEDGMENTS

The idea for the *Life Unstyled* book has been brewing for many years, at least as long as I've had my blog by the same name. Thanks to the success of my first two books, *Modern Rustic* and *Bohemian Modern*, my publisher Ryland Peters & Small finally let me loose on this idea and I have to keep pinching myself that it has finally come to fruition. Thank you to all at RPS: Cindy for believing in my idea; Jess for helping me find all these great homes; Annabel for helping me formulate my ideas and translate them into meaningful chapters, especially when I was having a tough time; Megan for listening to my design and layout ideas and making them better; and Leslie for all you do.

Having the brilliant Debi Treloar on my side made the whole experience an absolute dream. Debi, you are an incredible photographer, an easy-going travel partner, and an all-around inspiration. Thank you!

Thank you to all the homeowners in London, New York, France and Belgium. You bravely allowed us to photograph your gorgeous homes in their mostly natural state, without the usual over-styling that comes with a book shoot. I learned something valuable from each of you and I know that my readers will too.

To my friends and family spread across two continents, I'm grateful for your love and support in good times and bad. My sweet mum Jocelyn, who has supported me unconditionally over the years; my siblings Holly, Duncan and Eliott; my cousin Jordan; and my lovely in-laws. And, of course, my gorgeous little family, Ella, Johnny and Erick, who have watched me work so hard on this book and have given up a lot of family time together while I researched, travelled and wrote.

Finally, thank you so much to all my readers, whether you're just finding me now or are a loyal follower of my earlier books, blog and styling work. I hope *Life Unstyled* inspires you to create a home that you love and to be a bit gentler on yourself in the process. For continued inspiration for living a Life Unstyled, follow as I share my thoughts and snapshots of perfectly imperfect interiors at lifeunstyled.com and on Instagram/Twitter/Facebook, where I am @lifeunstyled.

INDEX

Page numbers in *italic* refer to the illustrations